What Really Matters

Conversation Starters for Men

by Everett J. Thomas
and J. Lorne Peachey

Faith & Life
Resources

Newton, Kansas
Scottdale, Pennsylvania
Waterloo, Ontario
Winnipeg, Manitoba

What Really Matters is the first volume in the series for men, Closer Than a Brother. The series was developed at the initiative, and with the financial support of Mennonite Men, which serves churches in the United States and Canada. For more information about Mennonite Men, write to: 722 Main, Newton, KS 67117-0347.
Website: www.mennonitemen.org

Unless otherwise noted, Scripture text is quoted, with permission, from the New Revised Standard Version, ©1989, Division of Christian Education of the National Council of Churches of Christ in the United States of America.

Hymn references and some prayers in this volume are taken, with permission, from *Hymnal: A Worship Book* © 1992 by Brethren Press, Elgin, Illinois; Faith & Life Press, Newton, Kansas, and Mennonite Publishing House, Scottdale, Pennsylvania.

Closer Than a Brother—Men's Series
WHAT REALLY MATTERS: CONVERSATION STARTERS FOR MEN
By Everett J. Thomas and J. Lorne Peachey

Copyright © 2002 by Faith & Life Resources, Scottdale, PA 15683
Published simultaneously in Canada by Faith & Life Resources, Waterloo, ON N2L 6H7
International Standard Book Number: 0-8361-9218-4
Printed in the United States of America
Book and cover design by Merrill R. Miller

To order books, or to request information, call 1-800-245-7894.
Website: www.mph.org

Table of contents

Welcome to this study!

By the time we reach middle age, most of us have established our identities, our families, and our spiritual foundation. As men, however, few of us have learned how to develop emotional and spiritual bonds with other men. This study booklet is designed to help you do that within a group of similarly committed Christian men as you talk about significant life issues.

You will be encouraged to find spiritual companionship that leaves you and another man "closer than a brother." If this doesn't click right away, don't worry. Be patient with yourself and your group mates. Still, this booklet assumes that as we work toward the goal of accountable relationships, we find we are also growing in our relationship with our Lord and brother, Jesus Christ.

Here's a preview of the study: Session 1, "Getting Our Bearings," will be more of a get-to-know-you time organized by your leader, perhaps around a meal. It will also get you thinking about spiritual companionship. Sessions 2 to 5 are a little more structured, and include suggestions for opening worship, study, and reflection exercises on the topics of friendship, money and power, sex, and family relationships. We hope these are meaningful times of spiritual growth and fellowship for you.

If you are the group leader ...

Please see the section, "How to use this booklet" and other notes in the "Leader's Guide" on page 41.

Getting Our Bearings

Spiritual companionship is an important way for men to grow personally as followers of Jesus.

When Jesus and his disciples met for their last supper together, it was obvious that they knew each other well. These friends had shared many meals together. We imagine those meals as times filled with simple joy and satisfaction with the bond they shared. And they would have been able to express delight in each other in ways that may seem startling to us today. Here is how the King James Version describes the interaction between Jesus and the disciple "whom Jesus loved":

> Now there was leaning on Jesus' bosom one of his disciples, whom Jesus loved. Simon Peter therefore beckoned to him, that he should ask who it should be of whom he spake. He then lying on Jesus' breast saith unto him, Lord, who is it? (John 13:23-25 KJV)

An arm's length culture
Most men today don't have this kind of intimacy; in fact, many flee from it because of certain connotations that North American society has imposed on it. Still, men can be nurtured as they find simple joy in each other's company. Simply

To the leader: Unlike subsequent chapters, this one does not include specific suggestions for worship and group activities. Guidance for planning this session is given in the leader notes on page 43.

being together must balance our tendency to drive ourselves to do things that are more clearly "productive."

We see rhythms of doing and being in Jesus' leadership of his disciples as they interact with the crowds, heal the sick, and debate with religious leaders. These times are followed by prayer and reflection—sometimes alone, sometimes in the company of friends. Such moments occur in the desert, on the Sea of Galilee, and around a dinner table.

This pattern of action and reflection carries with it the seeds of discipleship and accountability. As we observe actions in each others' lives, then spend time reflecting afterwards, a loyal and trusted friend can point out misjudgments and mistakes in our lives. He can also make us aware of how we are experiencing God and hearing the voice of God in ways we have not experienced before.

Privilege and power

Such accountability is especially important for men. In North American culture, we males are given special privileges and power simply because we are born male. For white men, these entitlements of power and privilege are greater than for people of color. By developing friendships and trust with other men, we find a safe context for addressing the stewardship of these privileges and power.

Spiritual companionship encourages us to manage these powers in ways that have integrity, working for the good of others and not just ourselves. We can let down our guard and begin to trust the counsel of a spiritual brother on matters that affect our lives deeply: (1) friendship, (2) wealth and power, (3) sex, and (4) family relationships.

Later booklets in this series will look at each topic in more depth. In this study, however, you will have opportunities to begin conversation about each of them at a more general level. Session 2 begins with male friendship, using the biblical story of King David and Jonathan. Session 3 focuses on wealth and power by looking at the example of Boaz in the book of Ruth. Session 4 considers sexual temptation, using the story of David and his illicit relationship with Bathsheba. The final session considers family relations by revisiting the story of Abraham and Sarah.

Our story: God's ears and mouthpiece

Spiritual companionship has been an important part of both our spiritual pilgrimages. It was in 1995 that we began intentionally talking with each other about what is happening to us spiritually and holding each other accountable for our relationship to God and to those around us. The Spirit led us to discover we were both hungry for a deeper walk as disciples. Out of this desire came a covenant to be spiritual companions.

What this means for us has grown and developed in the years since that beginning. Currently we talk together approximately every two weeks. We do this in person when we can. But because one of us lives in Indiana and the other in Pennsylvania, most of our conversations are by telephone, usually an hour and a half in length.

We ask each other questions about how we are experiencing the presence of God in our lives. We talk about the spiritual disciplines we are practicing (Bible study, prayer, diet, exercise) and about our relationships with our spouses, our families, and our congregations. We confess our sins to each other and prod each other to listen to the Spirit's nudging in our lives. We also rejoice with each other for the times of victory and joy, and sorrow for times of failure. For a list of the questions we ask each other, see the end of this chapter.)

In short, we are God's ears and mouthpiece—an awesome and joyous responsibility Christian brothers can have for each other.—*Everett & Lorne*

Finding a spiritual companion

The ultimate goal of this series is not simply to have lively group discussion in response to biblical illustrations. Our hope and prayer is that each one who participates will develop a spiritual companionship through which he will come to know God more intimately. Through such friendship, each will become accountable for how he lives as a disciple of Christ.

Each session will include opportunities—optional but encouraged—for you to talk honestly and openly with another man. Ideally, you will have the same partner throughout the study. This person may be someone you already know and trust, or it may be someone who becomes your confidant in the discussions. We hope that in these conversations with another, you will find

How to find a spiritual companion

Finding another man with whom to share your spiritual struggles and joys can be a scary experience, especially if you have not done so before. We hope that doing this study in a group context will make the process easier. Breaking into dyads gives you a chance to be open with another man in discussing a life issue. Your conversations may lead you to form an ongoing covenant of spiritual companionship. Here is how it might happen:

1. Pray about finding a spiritual companion.

2. Allow God's Spirit to work as your group breaks into twos to discuss the ideas in this book.

3. Be honest in your discussions with the man with whom you form a dyad, including how you relate to each other.

4. If the relationship that develops does not work, be open about what's happening and talk with your group leader about possible changes.

5. Allow the Spirit to work both with you and your spiritual companion as you discern if this could be a long-term relationship that will bring you both closer to God.

new levels of satisfaction and delight in your personal relationship with God and our divine brother, Jesus Christ.

Questions for spiritual companions

As you develop a spiritual companionship that goes beyond the conversation topics of this booklet, you may wish to use the following questions as you meet together:

1. **Encounters with God**
   a) How have you experienced God since we last talked?
   b) How have you been aware of God's love and grace?
   c) How do you find yourself resisting God?

2. **Spiritual disciplines**
   a) Have you spent meaningful time in prayer and meditation?
   b) Are you satisfied with your time spent in Bible reading/study?
   c) What other spiritual disciplines are you currently practicing?

3. **Family life**
   a) How would you describe your relationship with your spouse?
   b) How is your relationship with your children?
   c) Have you given priority time to your family?

4. **Relationship with congregation**
   a) Have you been faithful in attending activities of your congregation?
   b) How would you describe your relationship with your congregation?

5. Accountability

a) What sin do you need to confess?

b) Have you exposed yourself to any sexually explicit material or been with anyone in a compromising situation?

c) Have any of your financial dealings lacked integrity?

d) What else do you need to be accountable for?

6. Spiritual companionship

a) Is there anything about our relationship that you need to talk about?

b) Have you just lied to me?

Session 2

Friendship

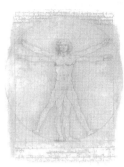

Forming deep bonds of friendship is emotionally healthy, and it can help us develop spiritual intimacy with Jesus.

Opening worship*

Song: "Great Is Thy Faithfulness" (*HWB* 327).

Guided prayer: Pray the following guided prayer together, with periods of silence between each sentence:

> Imagine a dry and parched land where a heavy dew brings relief and comfort in the morning. Imagine sunburned and cracked skin seared under the desert sun, and then a potion of oils lubricating and softening the face and hands. These are the images used to describe the special blessing we receive when we live in unity with our brothers. Imagine the desert of our busyness now being soothed by the balm of brotherly friendship.

Read Psalm 133.

Responsive prayer:
> Lord, we come before you,
>> not alone,
>> but in the company of one another.

Leader: Tips for leading the sessions are given on page 43.

**We share our happiness with each other,
and it becomes greater.**
We share our troubles with each other,
and they become smaller.
**We share one another's griefs and burdens,
and their weight becomes possible to
bear.**
May we never be too mean to give,
nor too proud to receive.
**For in giving and receiving
we learn to love and be loved;
we encounter the meaning of life,
the mystery of existence—
and discover you. Amen**

—Terry Falla, in *Be Our Freedom, Lord*, ed. by Terry Falla
(Adelaide: Lutheran Publishing House, 1984).

Exploring the topic

Boys in our culture are taught to be tough, inde-
pendent, resourceful, and self-assured. Even as
we grow into manhood, we are led to believe
that our emotions, or the feelings of others, must
never get in our way. This is the masculinity of
John Wayne, James Bond, and the beer-drinking,
smart-aleck hosts of "The Man Show" popular
on cable TV.

Maturing as men means we must move beyond
this view of masculinity. So it is that most men,
especially those who are married, spend much
of their twenties and thirties developing their
feminine side (see Food for thought 1, below).
This is a critical stage of development. It is during those years that we learn how to bond with
integrity to another person. For those who are
married, this happens most significantly with a
spouse. For those who are single, it happens
through significant friendships. And if we have

children, we learn to be nurturing and gentle. We are profoundly changed by the love which they return to us.

But some time after turning forty, healthy masculine development has us shift from the feminine side back into a deeper understanding of ourselves. This period of the "deep masculine" is quite different from the machismo and testosterone-driven masculinity of our teenage years. Having discovered emotional intimacy with spouse, children, or significant others, we are also now secure enough in our self-identity to experience emotional intimacy with other close friends. In doing so, we also strengthen the spiritual intimacy we have with our brother Jesus.

King Saul's son Jonathan was such a man. He knew how to be emotionally intimate with another man.

Read aloud 1 Samuel 18:1-5
Jonathan was a great man in his own right. By the time he met David, he had legendary achievements of his own about which to boast. In 1 Samuel 14, for example, Jonathan and his armor-bearer killed twenty warriors and panicked an entire Philistine garrison. Jonathan was also courageous and not afraid of saying what he thought. For example, he nonchalantly contravened the direct orders of his father, the unstable and irritable Saul (1 Sam. 14:24-46) and was saved from certain death only when the townspeople ransomed him.

But when Jonathan befriended David, he did so with no pretensions or ulterior motives. The son of a king, Jonathan might have been expected to make a play for the throne himself. Jonathan did just the opposite. He gave his royal robes to David, a poor sheepherder, along with his armor, his bow, and his belt. Time and time again, he saved David's life, sometimes at peril to his own.

The words used to describe the bond between these two friends are striking: "The soul of Jonathan was bound to the soul of David, and Jonathan loved him as his own soul" (18:1).

Food for thought 1: John the Beloved and John the Baptist

In the book *The Wild Man's Journey*, Catholic retreat master Richard Rohr and co-writer Joseph Martos describe the two journeys we take as men to find our way into the deep masculine.

The first journey occurs generally between the ages of twenty to forty. It might be called the journey of John the Beloved (see John 13:23a). This journey into the common feminine allows us to become increasingly comfortable with traditionally feminine strengths, such as listening, understanding, caring, and nurturing.

Young adult men who never take this first journey end with emotional and relational abilities frozen at a common masculine level. Some of us may know fifty-year-old men who still act like seventeen-year-olds. Their development is arrested in shallow masculinity, and they are incapable of emotional attachment with anyone else. They have never taken the journey of John the Beloved.

At about age forty, it is time to move on. After several decades of strengthening and exploring the feminine side, it is time for a second journey. This is the journey of John the Baptist, that wild man who lived on the edge of civilization eating from the land and wearing the hides of animals he killed.

Some men, unfortunately, make the first journey but never take this second journey. Consequently, they remain in the common feminine side the rest of their lives. This too is a form of arrested development; men stuck here can become self-protective, coddling, with too much inward energy and overdone relationships.

But when we take the journey of John the Baptist to the wild side, we do so equipped with lessons from that first journey of John the Beloved. The second journey leads to a deep and mature masculine quite different from the John Wayne masculinity of our youth. Here we learn to use the power and strength of the mature masculinity with which God has endowed us, but we do so integrating what we learned from our feminine side. Some call this the "wild man." This might also be what it means to be a "real gentleman."

Read aloud 1 Samuel 20:41-42

In this passage, Jonathan again saved David's life, but he also had to give him the bad news that Saul wanted to kill him. Jonathan urged David to flee for his life. This brief passage carries in it the heart of spiritual companionship: "The Lord shall be between me and you … forever." This is the context for developing a friend-

Food for thought 2: How we keep each other accountable

In 1995, Lorne and I began a pattern of accountability with each other that evolved into what we call "spiritual companionship" (see "Our Story," page 9). It began with a set of questions Lorne created from some earlier work he had done. About every other week, we took an hour to an hour and a half to work through these questions. Because we live in different states, it worked well to use the "free calls on Fridays" offered by a long-distance carrier. Other times we would schedule several hours to talk together if we were at the same meeting somewhere.

Eventually, the questions were altered to be even more pointed and specific (see page 11). It became impossible to avoid any subject because of the one question at the end of our sessions that we have come to both cherish and dread: "Have you just lied to me?" For us, lying includes the sin of omission.

After six years of this discipline, we now know exactly where the other may try to fudge a reply. We know the spots in each others' lives that we would rather not talk about. When I am tempted toward some vice or sin, it becomes a deterrent to know that Lorne will ask me specifically about it.

For example, several years ago I started buying lottery tickets occasionally. When the jackpot got large enough, I would buy $5 or $10 worth of tickets in hopes of winning $50 or $60 million. Lorne began asking me about this habit, and now, even when the jackpot hits $180 million, I ask myself: Do I really want to disappoint Lorne by admitting that I yielded to the temptation? There is no way I can go through our questions without him finding out—so I no longer buy lottery tickets.

We address graver issues than lottery tickets, of course. Specifically, we hold each other accountable for integrity in our marriage and family relationships. We ask directly about sexual temptations or vices that might find their way into other areas of our lives.

But the important question is always asked first: "How have you experienced God since we last talked?" Having a friend who knows me so well and who listens to my answers requires that I carefully and honestly review the progress, or lack thereof, in my walk with God in the preceding weeks.—*Everett*

ship bond that becomes holy. Sanctioned by God's presence, a spiritual companion becomes the voice and face of God.

David eventually became the greatest king in ancient Israel. One can easily believe that the spiritual companionship he experienced with Jonathan was one of the reasons for his success.

Talking it through

In groups of two, consider these questions in relation to the biblical story and what we have included in this chapter:

1. As you read about the friendship of David and Jonathan, what emotions do you experience: envy? peace? frustration? scandal? Why?

2. Do you have a relationship with another man somewhat comparable to the friendship of David and Jonathan? Why or why not?

3. Would you like to have such a relationship? What are the next steps you might take to help make this happen?

4. Where do you find yourself on the masculine journey—with John the Beloved? John the Baptist? Or are you somewhere in between?

After twenty or thirty minutes, gather again in the larger group. If you feel free, share one new thing you have learned in this session, or tell the group of a change you would like to make in your life as a result of this study.

Closing

Friendship can be an important reminder of the ultimate friendship we can have with our Savior and brother, Jesus Christ. To celebrate this friendship, sing the hymn "What a Friend We Have in Jesus" (*HWB* 573 or 574).

Sit in silence for a few minutes. Then listen as the following passages are read from the book of Proverbs from the New Living Translation:

> Disregarding another person's faults preserves love; telling about them separates close friends (17:9).

> There are "friends" who destroy each other, but a real friend sticks closer than a brother (18:24).

> Wounds from a friend are better than many kisses from an enemy (27:6).

> A friend is always loyal, and a brother is born to help in time of need (17:17).

Conclude the session with a time of open prayer. Share brief prayers as you wish before the leader concludes with a closing prayer.

Session 3

Money and Power

In the middle years, men are at the peak of their power, wealth, and influence. God calls us to use these gifts to bring life to others.

Opening worship

Song: "God Whose Giving" (*HWB* 383) or "Now Thank We All Our God" (*HWB* 86).

Scripture reading: Read Psalm 1 aloud in the New International Version.

Prayer:
> Gracious God, all of life is a gift from you.
> All we are finds its source in your creative
>   Spirit.
>
> Dispel the darkness of our selfish ambition,
>   our quest to lord it over others,
>   our lust for the things of this world.
>
> Enable us to use our talents, our resources,
>   our being
> To extend your reign in our world.
> Through Jesus Christ our Lord. Amen

Leader: Tips for leading the sessions are given on page 43.

Exploring the topic

Most of us will experience a transition sometime between our forties and sixties. For some, this will be a mid-life crisis. But these can also be wonderful years when we experience stability, achievement at various levels, and credibility with our peers.

Something else also begins to take place within us. Now that we've reached many of our goals, with fewer dreams left to chase, we begin to consider our mortality. "What difference will it make that I lived in this world for part of a century?" we ask ourselves. "What are the things that I am doing now that will matter in light of eternity?"

These musings are often accompanied by yearnings to be a genuine blessing to those around us. Jungian scholars describe this as "king energy." When we are able to express this energy appropriately, then our efforts bring health and life to others. Family, colleagues, acquaintances—all are strengthened and blessed by our presence.

A vivid picture of this stewardship of energy occurs in the book of Ruth. Ruth, a foreign widow who has returned to Israel with her mother-in-law Naomi, has been gleaning in the fields of Boaz, seeking ways to support herself and her mother-in-law. Boaz becomes a provider of blessing to her.

Read aloud Ruth 3:1-13

At the point in this story where Ruth makes plain her intention to Boaz, she makes a curious request: "Spread your cloak over your servant, for you are next-of-kin."

This simple sentence reveals layers of cultural practice. When a man died without fathering a son in Ancient Near Eastern culture, the man's closest brother or relative was expected to marry the widow so that she might bear a son. This son, then, became the descendant of the dead man, not the descendant of the biological father. All of the dead man's estate passed to the son.

Furthermore, if the man who died was also poor (as was the case with Ruth's husband), then the next of kin was expected to share his estate with the boy, so that the dead man's lineage could continue. In such a system, one's power and wealth could be referred to as a "cloak" or "skirt."

So on that threshing floor when Ruth startled a sleeping Boaz by uncovering his legs (probably a euphemism for "genitals"), she was requesting that Boaz spread his wealth and procreative powers over her.

The sensuality of this scene notwithstanding, what Ruth requested was a serious financial matter for Boaz. To his credit, and apparently without hesitation, he immediately agreed to grant her request.

"And now, my daughter, do not be afraid," Boaz responded. "I will do for you all that you ask, for all the assembly of my people know that you are a worthy woman." In the phrase "my people," Boaz signals that although Ruth is a foreigner, he will be an advocate for her, using all the power and influence at his disposal. Boaz is willing to reward her because of her impeccable morality. In so doing, he does not hesitate to risk

the wealth of his estate. However, there is first
the matter of a closer next of kin to be considered.

Read aloud Ruth 4:1-6
The scene at the village gate (where legal trans-
actions occur) is delicious in its drama. First, the
next of kin, whose name may be understood as
a derisive "so-and-so," stops at the assembly of
village elders gathered by Boaz. Boaz tells the
next of kin about a field belonging to Naomi
and points out that the next of kin has first
chance at "redeeming" it.

The man is eager to acquire more property and
agrees to purchase it. Now Boaz tests the man's
integrity. He explains that there is a young
Moabite woman who also belongs to Naomi
and that the woman must go with the field. The
hapless man is caught. He knows that if he buys
the field, he will have to divide his estate with
any son born to Ruth. Sheepishly he changes

Food for thought 1: Ruth's grit

The book of Ruth is a hymn of praise
to the faithfulness of one young
Moabite woman. As a widow with no
man to provide for her in this Ancient
Near Eastern world, Ruth chose a
dangerous course for her life. She
would leave the relative security of
her homeland and family and accom-
pany her mother-in-law back to
Naomi's hometown of Bethlehem in
Israel. When Naomi objected, Ruth
declared, "Your people shall be my
people, and your God my God"
(1:16b).

As an old widow beyond childbear-
ing age, there was no safety net for
Naomi; starvation would be the likely
result of the journey alone to Israel.
On the other hand, the young and
attractive widow Ruth would be vul-
nerable to mistreatment by young
men wishing to make sport of her,
especially since she was a foreigner.
But Naomi's only hope for survival
was for Ruth to marry and have a
son. The story of Ruth is one of self-
lessness and faithfulness. She was
willing to give her life and procreative
powers to ensure that the old woman
Naomi would live.

his mind, so he turns to Boaz and says, "Take my right of redemption yourself." Boaz does.

This transaction at the village gate, sealed as usual by the exchange of a sandal, demonstrates the use of wealth and power at its best. The mature Boaz, moved by the faithfulness and moral rectitude of a young, foreign woman, blessed her by redeeming her into full citizenship in the nation of Israel.

In return for Boaz's willingness to spread his cloak over Ruth, God spreads his cloak over them both. Within three generations, this marriage gives Israel the greatest king in the Old Testament. Ruth and Boaz become the great grandparents of King David.

Talking it through

Share in twos: Consider the following questions, which are designed to help you move from analysis of the Boaz story to openness about your life and focus on the way you use your wealth and power today.

Food for thought 2: To share is to bless

To be blessed by another man—and to share in another man's power—can be an enriching and energizing experience. It happened to me in 1995 at the conclusion of the joint sessions of the General Conference Mennonite Church (GC) and the Mennonite Church (MC) in Wichita, Kansas.

Delegates at that session had just voted to explore joining these two groups. As I was preparing to leave, I met Vern Preheim, a key leader in the merger discussions, at the elevators of the Broadmore Hotel. "Lorne," he said, "I want you to know that I believe the MC delegates voted for integration in large part because of your work and your support as editor of *Gospel Herald*."

In that moment, I experienced incredible blessing, not only from Vern, but also through Vern from God. Vern's generosity taught me that I too can share the power God has given me. It is in that sharing that I can bless and be a blessing to other men.—*Lorne*

1. Which qualities of Boaz do you see in each other, or in another man in your group, or in someone else you know?

2. Share with each other times in your life when you feel you responded in a Boaz-like way.

3. Share about the opportunities you see in your life today where you could be a Boaz but worry about the risk to your wealth and influence.

Share with the larger group as you feel free:
What have you learned about yourself through the story of Boaz? What have you learned about your discussion partner(s). This discussion should be open but not violate confidences or go beyond the comfort level of the men who share.

After all have had the opportunity to share, the leader leads in a group prayer, citing the specific examples that were shared and asking God's blessing on each person.

Closing
Have one member read Psalm 1:1-3 aloud, with the group responding "Blessed is the Man" after each verse.

Song: "Forth in Thy Name" (*HWB* 415) or another appropriate closing.

Session 4

Sex

Sexuality is a gift of God. Like many of God's gifts it can be corrupted by misuse, or it can be a source of true joy when celebrated as God meant it to be, within a faithful marriage covenant.

Opening worship

Song: "For the Beauty of the Earth" (*HWB* 89)— first four verses only.

Meditation exercise:

Relax in your chair, close your eyes, and take several deep breaths. Then listen as one person reads Song of Solomon 7:1-12. During the reading let your imagination run. At the end of the reading, silently ponder these questions:

- What happened in your mind and in your body during this reading?

- How do you feel about the fact that such explicit sexual imagery comes from the Bible?

Leader: Tips for leading the sessions are given on page 43.

- Is sex a gift from God for which you are thankful? Or is it a part of your life that causes more anxiety and frustration than joy?

Prayer:

Come, O Holy Spirit, O Sanctifying Spirit,
> fill our hearts,
> fill our lives
> with the feel of your fiery presence,
> so that all we do,
> all that we are,
> comes from you within us.
> Amen.

Exploring the topic

No doubt about it, the fires of sexuality still burn
for middle adult men (40-60). For some, it may
be without the wild abandon we once knew in
our youth. Others of us are well aware of our sex
drive well into mature adulthood—increasing, if
not in frequency, at least in intensity.

Whether we are with those who find themselves
thinking less about sex than in their youth, or
with those who have an intensified desire for
sexual expression, one thing is certain: As
Christian men we are faced with temptations
related to sex. Being a man of fidelity and purity
has never been easy, but in our North American
culture today, obsession with sex brings with it
many opportunities to turn from God's will and
follow the path of sin.

All of us can do stupid things to prove to ourselves that we are still virile or to secure the
adventures we want. We might titillate ourselves
by venturing into adult bookstores or onto
pornography Web sites. We might feed our fantasy life by visiting a shopping mall or other

public place and amuse and arouse ourselves with flirtation.

Sadly, some men need to prove to themselves that they still have sexual prowess. Others may be looking for sexual adventure and find attraction in the forbidden. Too often both groups end up having an illicit affair like King David's.

Read aloud 2 Samuel 11:1-5
It was spring. David was rejoicing in the victory that his army had over the Ammonites. His men had besieged the enemy town of Rabbah.

After a fine afternoon nap, David walked along the roof of his palace. His eyes happened onto the beautiful Bathsheba bathing herself on her rooftop. The text is careful to point out that her menstrual period was over. David would have recognized the ritual of purification and perhaps assumed this was the time in her cycle for safe sex.

Bathsheba may have been bathing innocently on that rooftop, or she may have been practicing the same adroit moves we see later in her life (see sidebar 1). Regardless, David could not resist the temptation before him. As monarch, he held the power, and Bathsheba responded, whether from fear or from desire. David invited her to his palace, had sex with her, and then arranged to have her husband killed. He covered up the affair by marrying Bathsheba.

When the innocent boy born of their illicit liaison died, David grieved this loss as God's punishment for his actions. He fasted and prayed to save the boy's life. But when God ignored his pleas, David accepted his punishment without complaining or making excuses for himself. He knew he deserved the punishment that came his way.

Read aloud 2 Samuel 12:15b-25
As men, it's easy for us to identify with David's drive for sex. While we may not have taken the actions David did, we can understand how he came to them. David saw a beautiful woman bathing, invited her to his place for a one-night stand, and then sent her home. He apparently had never met her before the day they had sex. Their initial relationship was not a personal one that eventually flowered into appropriate physical contact. Their relationship on the first day of their acquaintance was similar to the promiscuity today's television shows and movies attempt to titillate us with.

Despite all this, however, God allowed the relationship to flourish. After their firstborn (and unnamed) son died, David consoled Bathsheba with sex that apparently had God's approval. At

---

Food for thought 1: Bathsheba's legacy

Later appearances by Bathsheba suggest that she was an intelligent woman fully engaged in the world around her. In 1 Kings 1, Bathsheba played a key role in Solomon's dramatic succession to the throne. In that setting, in collaboration with the prophet Nathan (the same prophet who first condemned David's illicit affair with her), the two skillfully manipulated the dying King David to anoint Bathsheba's son Solomon to succeed him as king.

The last time we see Bathsheba (1 Kings 2), she is the Queen Mother and, as such, responsible for King Solomon's harem. In this episode, Bathsheba adroitly carries a message to Solomon that would immediately get Solomon's most powerful rival killed! Somehow, Bathsheba manages to show up at the most important moments in the dynastic succession of Israel's kings. Consequently, she became the most important wife of ancient Israel's greatest king and mother to its wisest.

least the Bible tells us God loved the second son that this union produced (v. 24).

While we must be careful in how we interpret the David and Bathsheba story, it does show us what happens when sexual energy is used for selfish and immoral purposes: sin and death. At the same time, sexual energy used in right relationship produces consolation, joy, and creativity. The fruit of David and Bathsheba's second, righteous, relationship was King Solomon, the second most important king in the Old Testament.

As Christian men, we need to covenant with each other not to follow our sexual temptations into an illicit affair as David did. And we need to ask ourselves and each other: When could our sexual adventures and the fruits of our passions end in sin and death , and when do they end in blessing an important relationship in our lives?

Pornography, sexually explicit jokes or stories, flirtation, hours spent weaving fantasies into hopes for reality, even contact that is physically arousing but stops short of intercourse—all these are issues for which we need to set boundaries for ourselves as followers of Jesus Christ. We must be accountable to God, to ourselves, and to each other for the ways in which we use and express our sexual desires.

Talking it through
Discussing the issues raised in this session may be difficult for men in your group, particularly if they do not know each other well. Begin by pondering individual answers to the following questions:

1. What is your reaction to the story of the David and Bathsheba affair? Disgust? Sorrow? Or do you find yourself envying David just a bit for his adventure that did not completely estrange him from God in the long run? Why do you react the way you do?

2. What is the role of sexual fantasy in your life? How do you control it? What about masturbation?

3. Overall, do you find your sexuality a joyous part of who you are, or does it cause you more anxiety and distress than joy?

Food for thought 2: Confessing our sins to each other

In my work as a spiritual director, I have learned that issues about sex will inevitably come up when one talks to men about their relationship with God. For example, one man needed to talk about something that had been troubling him for more than twenty-five years.

"After my wife and I were married," he told me, "we became friends with another couple interested in 'open marriages,' a concept common in the anti-establishment 1960s. This couple gave us books to read and told us they would be interested in such an arrangement with us."

My friend's wife was not interested, but he was attracted to the other woman and heavily tempted by the forbidden offered through such an adventure. "When my wife found out about my lack of faithfulness, she was devastated," the man said. He described what happened as "a holocaust for our relationship."

Although intercourse was not involved, it did include the inappropriate fondling and kissing. "That was clearly a violation of my marriage covenant," my friend confessed to me. "It not only hurt my wife, but it permanently damaged our relationship with that couple."

"I've not been able to confess this to anyone before," my friend said. For twenty-five years, he held onto that sin—far too long to wait for confession. But there was nowhere in the church he felt safe to reveal his secret and come clean before God.

With sexual sin, men need to do more than just confess to God. While that is an important step, too often we do not realize God's forgiveness or forgive ourselves until we have unburdened ourselves to another. "Confess your sins to one another," James writes (5:16). These must include our sexual sins.—Lorne

4. What do you want to do differently in your sexual life as the result of having studied the story of David and Bathsheba?

Break into dyads, preferably those formed earlier. In turn, pick one question from the list above that you are comfortable discussing with your partner. If you are not comfortable with these questions, talk about why.

After 15-20 minutes of discussion in dyads, gather again in the larger group and share as you feel free. What have you learned through the story of David and Bathsheba? What do you

---

Food for thought 3: What about self-gratification?

Likely the most common but least talked about issue related to sex is masturbation. If folklore is to be believed, 99 per cent of men say they do it, and the other 1 percent lie! While that perception may be more an attempt at justification than a description of reality, one thing is certain: masturbation is a subject men find difficult to talk about.

Yet we need to do so. When Lorne edited *With* magazine for youth in the early 70s, he ran an article titled, "What About Masturbation?" The letters he received in response were the most he ever received on one topic in thirty years of editing in the Mennonite church. Clearly men of all ages wanted to talk about the issue and its effect on their lives.

We have found that when men are really honest with each other about their sexuality, the subject of masturbation usually finds its way into the conversation. Talking about this issue is one way we come to a resolve what role, if any, masturbation has in our lives. Do we believe, for example, that masturbation is a gift from God to help us manage our sexual drives? Or do we identify the practice with the hidden faults and secret sins that get mentioned in prayers and sermons?

Each of us must come to our decision about masturbation. We do so, first of all, in prayer. But we believe that this subject must also be part of what gets discussed in an honest spiritual companionship in which both men seek to know God better.

want to do differently in your life? This discussion should be open but not violate confidences or go beyond the comfort level of the persons involved.

Closing

Read together these selected verses from Genesis 1:27-31 (from the New Living Translation):

> God created people in his own image;
> God patterned them after himself;
> male and female he created them.
> God blessed them and told them,
> "Multiply and fill the earth...."
> Then God looked over all he had made,
> And he saw that it was excellent in every
>   way.

Sit together in a period of silent meditation and prayer. After three or four minutes, invite those who wish to pray short audible prayers to do so.

Song: "If All You Want, Lord." (*HWB* 512) If the tune is unfamiliar, the leader may want to read the hymn to the group.

Session 5

Family

It is through family that both our DNA and our values are passed on to the coming generations. Our families have special meaning, however, when we see our true worth and value as coming from God and the family of faith.

Opening worship

Song: "Lord of the Home" (*HWB* 490).

Think about your brothers:
Look around the room at each one present. Visualize every person as a sibling in your family of origin. This is what it means for us each to be a child of God. The true family to which a Christian belongs is a spiritual one, not a biological one. The families into which we were born and the families in which we live now are not the ones to which we owe final allegiance. Jesus calls us into a spiritual family, and that calling influences the way we relate to the biological families we are a part of.

Leader: Tips for leading the sessions are given on page 43.

Prayer:
> God of love and justice,
> > we long for peace within and peace without.
> We long for harmony in our families,
> > for serenity in the midst of struggle,
> > and for commitment to each other's growth.

We long for the day when our homes
will be a dwelling place for your love.

Yet we confess that we are often anxious;
     we do not trust each other,
     and we harbor violence.
We are not willing to take the risks
     and make the sacrifices that love
requires.

Look upon us with kindness and grace.
Rule in our homes and in all the world;
     show us how to walk in your paths,
     through the mercy of our Savior. Amen

—from *HWB* 696

Exploring the topic

As we reach middle age, many of us begin to
think of posterity. If we have children, we
become aware that it is through them that our
DNA will remain in humankind's gene pool.
Some of us have adopted children; they carry
into future generations the values and convic-
tions we have taught them. Some of us are single; still we seek to leave our mark through our
relationships with the next generations through
mentoring and teaching. Some essence of ourselves will continue on after we are gone.

Abraham knew about the importance of children. In Abraham's Ancient Near Eastern world,
the worst fate that could befall a man was to die
without children—especially sons. The best fate
would be to have children and grandchildren
too numerous to count. Well into his mature
years, little mattered to Abraham as much as
the fact that he was poor in posterity. Abraham
and his beloved wife Sarah grieved that their

lineage apparently would not be carried on. However, in their older years, God gave them a son, Isaac, and through Isaac, they learned much about what family ultimately means.

Read aloud Genesis 21:1-4, 8
Isaac was born to Sarah, who once had laughed at the first thought of her elderly womb conceiving and bearing a child (Gen. 18:1-15). Sarah too was vindicated in the eyes of her contemporaries when she finally gave birth.

Just as for Abraham, our families are us. Many of us have weathered years of ups and downs with our own beloved Sarahs. The children that spring from this companionship carry the essence of our existence. They often define a major portion of who we are. Our children look and act so much like us that it scares and sometimes embarrasses us. They reveal to the whole world some things about ourselves that we would prefer to keep hidden. They represent (re-present) us to the world.

But families are not the end-all of life with God. In fact, family can become more important than God. When that happens, God may test our priorities. He tested Abraham, and Abraham's response has been celebrated for millennia as a model of faithfulness.

Read aloud Genesis 22:1-3, 9-12
Child sacrifice was common to the religions surrounding Abraham in this Ancient Near Eastern world. It was the most radical kind of firstfruits offerings: the sacrifice of the fruits of one's own loins.

God asked Abraham to give up the one thing that he loved most: himself. Did Abraham love God more than he loved his "self" that would be passed along through young Isaac to his descendants? To his eternal credit, Abraham loved God so much that he was willing to give up his only begotten son. Because of this incident, the children of Israel would never again countenance such a practice in their religious activities.

Two thousand years later, of course, this same God so loved the world that he gave up his only begotten son (John 3:16). Through Jesus' death on the cross, God demonstrated that he was willing to give us more than he ever expects of us. Through this act, which demonstrated God's radical love and devotion toward us, those who believe in Jesus become God's posterity and part of God's family. At times, we are called to choose between our biological family and God's family.

Food for thought 1: Brothers in the family of God

As a boy, I was enamored with the Passover story for ignoble reasons. I was the second born in a family of six children, and I very much felt my secondary status. I knew that my father had been the firstborn in his family as had my mother in hers. My secondary status was evident all around. Then one day in Sunday school, while we were studying the Exodus 12 story, I suddenly deduced that if the Egyptian Passover came again, my father, my mother, and my older brother would be gone and I would be in charge!

My sense of disenfranchisement as a second born was so strong that I even struggled with the fact that Jesus was God's firstborn. The experience in my family of origin was such that I wondered if God would ever value me as much as others. I was literally jealous of Jesus.

But the day I was baptized, my secondary status changed for me. My father offered me a new way of understanding the family of God. He said to me, "I may still be your earthly father, but in the church we are brothers now with the same heavenly father."—*Everett*

Read aloud Mark 3:31-35

This leads us to the question of family. Is our biological family more important than our faith in God? Is the family we sired (or wish we could sire) more important than the family of God created by God's Isaac-sacrifice of Jesus? What does it mean to be so faithful that we are willing, even, to move our family members and their needs to second priority? If God is calling us to give up this most sacred part of our lives, would we respond as Abraham did?

Talking it through

Break into dyads (preferably those formed earlier in the previous sessions) and work together on the following questions:

1. How important is posterity to you? What examples from your life can you give about how its importance affects how you live and the things you do?

Food for thought 2: Firstfruits of the loins

In our world, body piercing and tattoos are still considered by many to be signs of the counterculture. In Abraham's Ancient Near Eastern world, when the rite of circumcision came with the covenant between Abraham and God as described in Genesis 17, this practice would also have been viewed as counterculture.

Abraham's world floated on a cashless economy. A man's wealth was measured by the number of children, wives, servants, and flocks that he accumulated. Consequently, a man's ability to create life out of his loins was his real power and the source of his wealth. These ancients believed that the sperm carried the seed of a human being and the womb was simply the garden into which the seed was planted. A man's genitals were, indeed, the family jewels.

The covenant of circumcision that God made with Abraham, then, centered on the core of Abraham's existence, success, power, and wealth. Through this practice, Abraham and his descendants literally gave the first piece of themselves and their most important asset to God. In this way, God received the firstfruits of a man's reproductive power, and all subsequent fruit of his loins was then under God's blessing.

2. What is your response to the story of God asking Abraham to sacrifice Isaac? How would you respond were you asked to do something similar?

3. Circumcision is no longer required of the children of God. But how do you give back to God the firstfruits of who you are?

4. Are there areas of your life or ways in which you have had to put the family of God before your family of origin?

After twenty to thirty minutes, gather as a larger group and as you feel comfortable, share what you have learned about yourself and your view of family. What is the growing edge for you in relating to your family? To God?

Closing

This marks the end of this study on issues that matter to men. Take some time to reflect on what you have learned. What goals have you set for yourself as the result of this study?

What have you learned about spiritual companionship? What are some highlights of the time you spent listening, praying, and attending to the needs of another. Were you able to form lasting spiritual companionships? What are the next steps you would like to take?

Take time to pray for each other in the group.

Song: "For the Beauty of the Earth" (*HWB* 89).

Closing prayer:
God of community,
whose call is more insistent

than ties of family or blood;
may we so respect and love
those whose lives are linked with
ours
that we fail not in loyalty to you,
but makes choices according to your
will,
through Jesus Christ. Amen

—From *HWB* 736

Leader's Guide

How to use this booklet

This booklet is designed so that each partici-
pant can have his own copy. The book should
be used for participation in the group (for example, the responsive readings and discussion
questions), and for personal reflection and
growth between sessions. As leader, encourage
the men to read the session articles ahead of
time, and to bring their books to the sessions.

Later in this leader's section there are notes for
leading each session. Pay special attention to
the introductory session, because it requires that
you tailor the booklet material to your group. For
sessions 2-5, be sure to check the individual session notes below, as well as the following hints
on the flow of the sessions:

Opening and closing worship
You will likely want to adapt the opening worship and closing exercises to fit the needs of
your group. If you are not a singing group, you
may want to use the words of the hymns in some
other way, or use other appropriate openings.
Have hymnals available as appropriate.

Exploring the topic
If the men do not read the material ahead of
time, you should be prepared to present the con-

tent of the articles to the men as a lead-in to the section, "Talking it through." The articles are short enough that you may read them aloud together. Ideally, however, the material should be read ahead of time, or should be presented more informally than simply reading it.

Thinking it through: dyads and close-to-home conversation

The sessions often call the group to break into dyads for sharing. We also encourage men to remain in the same dyad through all the sessions, so that they can begin to experience the benefits of spiritual companionship. However, you must discern how far your group is ready to go with the use of dyads. If your group does not know each other well, dyads may feel threatening to some when they are asked to talk more personally about themselves.

You are encouraged to push out the group's comfort zones, but don't force it. If your group does not feel ready to try dyads, ask them to meet in groups of three or four and/or to talk less personally about the same issues. This is better than no discussion at all. However, as the sessions continue, you may challenge them to be bolder in their sharing. Also, if some want to meet in dyads and others do not, consider having a "two-track" system, with some dyads, and some larger groups.

Notes for individual sessions

Session 1: Getting Our Bearings

We suggest that you use this session primarily as a get-to-know-you time, especially if you have not been together as a group before. Try meeting together over a meal—a barbecue, or at a restaurant. Take plenty of time to have participants share a little about their work, their family, and their faith journeys. Then take about thirty minutes for the more formal part of the gathering:

The agenda is short, but very important. Your tasks are:

1. Introduce one of the main goals of this study: to learn to talk about men's issues in a safe, Christian environment, and in so doing, to grow as disciples of Jesus Christ.

2. Review the main topics coming up in the next four sessions.

3. Introduce spiritual companionship. Here, present the material in the introductory chapter. Ask the men to react to the idea of spiritual companionship. What are the barriers? What could be the benefits? How ready are they to risk such a relationship?

4. Encourage men to find a conversation partner for the next studies. Explain that these dyads may be experienced differently in the group. Some may evolve into a more mature spiritual companionship. Some may not work from the beginning, and may need to be reconfigured early on. Some dyads may work fine for the next four sessions, then may motivate the

men to find spiritual companionship with other friends for the future.

You will need to be flexible and sensitive to the group's comfort zone. If your presentation on spiritual companionship doesn't break down any reserve the men have, you may need to conduct the study relying on discussion groups of three or four men, rather than dyads.

After you have decided how to structure your conversation groups, close the gathering with a time of prayer, asking God to guide your group as they grow spiritually through this experience.

Session 2: Friendship

Opening worship: Guided prayer is a meditative exercise of the imagination, in which participants open themselves to God's activity in their hearts. To do this well, you should invite each man to sit comfortably and relax with eyes closed and mind attentive. Read the paragraph slowly, allowing pauses between each clause so that the pictures can fix themselves in the minds of the men. Finish with a time of silent prayer before reading Psalm 133.

Encourage the men to read the entire book of Ruth in preparation for Session 2. It takes about fifteen minutes in one setting.

Session 3: Wealth and Power

While participants are encouraged to read the chapters before every session, it may be especially important for the next session (Session 4), which is on sex. Remember to announce this in the session—perhaps at the beginning, and again at the end as a reminder.

Session 4: Sex

Remember to create a relaxed atmosphere for the meditation exercise in the opening worship.

As we indicated in the chapter, sexuality can be a hard topic to talk about at a deep level—especially if we have experienced personal brokenness in this area. However, if that is the case, enormous growth and healing can come if we can become free to talk about it with trusted mentors and friends.

We have tried to make the discussion time easier by asking that each person choose only one topic for discussion, according to their comfort level. Emphasize that it is their choice, and that they also have the option of not sharing with each other on the topic and may, instead, discuss what it is that keeps them from discussing it.

Session 5: Family

Since this is the final session, you may wish to take some time, either at the end of this session, or in an extra session, to summarize what you have learned and to plan next steps. Consider using the other booklets in the Closer Than a Brother Series as they are released (call Faith & Life Resources at 800 743-2484 for more information). Or develop your group through the resource *Momentum*, available from Mennonite Men (316 283-5100; 722 Main, Newton, KS 67117-0347. Website: www.mennonitemen.org).

Notes

Notes

Closer Than a Brother
Men's Series

What Really Matters: Conversation Starters for Men
Available in May 2002

Men can grow in discipleship by being in a group with other Christian men. This study invites men to develop relationships of emotional and spiritual intimacy with each other, encourages them to work at accountability with another man, and provides an overview of the topics of the rest of the series—Friendship, Money & Power, Sex, and Family/Relationships.

Closer Than a Brother: Building Deeper Friendships
Available in early 2003

Many men desire deeper friendships, but don't know how to begin. This study provides opportunity to reflect on friendship while encouraging group experiences that foster such friendships.

The Meaning of Tough: Using Power and Wealth
Available in spring 2003

Despite changes in gender roles, men must still grapple with how to manage the money they earn and the power they have in their homes, churches, and workplaces. Like sex, wealth and power can be abused or used responsibly, and in a God-honoring way.

Sex and Faith: Celebrating God's Gifts
Available in summer 2003

Men think about sex a great deal. Some feel they are not getting enough, some get too much. Many have questions about appropriate and healthy habits of thought and action and don't know how to talk about them constructively. This study will help Christian men learn how to honor God through their sexuality.

Relatively Speaking: Strengthening Family Ties
Available in summer 2003

Men relate to families as sons, brothers, fathers, and members of extended families. This study goes beyond the patriarchal and hierarchical models of family in discussing the vital roles of fathers and husbands, and also acknowledges the needs of single men.

Faith & Life
Resources